KATIE MELUA_ PIECE BY PIECE

D1493677

C014019889

Piano transcriptions by Derek Jones and Mike Batt
from original arrangements by Mike Batt.

Published by

DRAMATICO

MUSIC PUBLISHING LTD.
PO Box 214, Farnham, Surrey, GU10 5XZ

www.dramatico.com

ISMN M-9002985-4-6

Shy Boy

Words & Music by Mike Batt

If you___ on - ly knew___ you could make your dreams___ come true.___

___ All___ you got - ta do is ask___ me to.___ 3. If

this was a quiz on a T. V. show and the prize was a guy who would
4. Some guys act a bit too sure and may - be you're think - in' that less___

love me so,___ what - ev - er they ask,___ the an - swer I know.___
___ is more,___ but Ho - ney you still___ got - ta knock on my door.___

5

Nine Million Bicycles

Words & Music by Mike Batt

it's a thing___ we can't de-ny,___ like the fact that I___ will love you 'til I die.

We are twelve bil - lion light_ years from the edge.

That's a guess,___ no - one can ev - er say it's true,___ but I know that I___ will al-ways be with you. I'm

Piece By Piece

Words & Music by Katie Melua

I'll shed like skin_____ our me-mo-ries of la-zy days,_____ and fade a-way the sha- dow of your face._____

Ooh._____ Ooh._____

Ooh._____ Ooh._____

15

Half Way Up The Hindu Kush

Words & Music by Katie Melua / Mike Batt

1. The first time that I saw you___ I said: "For good-ness' sake, that
(2.) next time that I saw you,___ you looked in-to my eyes. I was

man's___ got the pow-er, he's a charm-er___ with a snake."
sit-ting on your car-pet___ when I felt it___ be-gin to rise.

half - way up the Hin - du,____ from half - way up the Hin - du____ Kush.____

20

Blues In The Night

Words by John Mercer
Music by Harold Arlen

and when the sweet talk-ing's done._____ A man is a two - face,_____ a

wor - ri - some thing who'll leave you to sing the blues_____

rubato

_____ in the night."_____

My ma - ma done told me._____

27

Spider's Web

Words & Music by Katie Melua

1. If a black man is ra - cist,___ is___ it O - kay?
2. I could tell you___ to___ go to war,

If it's a white man's ra - ci - sm that___ made him that way?___ 'Cos the
or I could march for peace and___ fight - ing no more.___ But how do

30

-a - no keys are black and white, but they

sound like a mil-lion col-ours in your mind.

The pi -

-a - no keys are black and white, but they sound like a mil-lion col-ours in your mind,

they sound like a mil-lion col-ours in your mind.

Blue Shoes

Words & Music by Mike Batt

1. These blue shoes seem to suit me well, when I feel like hell, as I do now that you're gone.
2. You and I made the per-fect pair, it don't seem fair, I loved you more than you know.
3. These blue shoes seem to suit my soul, since you shot that hole, shot that hole in my heart.

Lost and lone-ly since
Sor-ry I'm in such a
And if I wind up on the

D.S. al Coda I

Coda I

36

I've been wear-ing my blue shoes.

On The Road Again

Words and Music by Alan Wilson and Floyd Jones

1. Well I'm so_____ tired of cry-ing but I'm out
(2.) first time I tra - velled out___
(Verses 4 & 5 see block lyric)

_____ on the road_ a - gain,_____ well I'm so___
_____ in the rain and snow,_____ (in the rain and snow), you know the

Well, I'm so_____ tired of cry - ing but I'm out_____

Thankyou, Stars

Words & Music by Mike Batt

Some call_ it faith,_ some call it love._ Some call_ it gui - dance from a-bove.

_ You are_ the rea - son we found ours, so

thank - you_ stars._

Some peo - ple think_ it's far a - way,_ some know it's with_ them ev -'ry day.

— You are_ the rea - son we found ours, so

thank - you_ stars._

own   it's the   way back home.

Just Like Heaven

Words by Robert Smith
Music by Robert Smith, Simon Gallup, Porl Thompson, Boris Williams & Laurence Tolhurst

I Cried For You

Words & Music by Katie Melua

feel that ma gic in your hand. To me you're like a wild rose, they nev-er un - der-stood, why
love of ours or that we met. They may not know how much you meant to me.

I cried for you____ when the sky cried for you,____ and when you went I be-came a hope-less

drift- er.

But this life was not for you____ though I learned from you,

____ that beau-ty need on - ly be a whis - per.

I Do Believe in Love

Words & Music by Katie Melua

You might think it's strange, _____ for all___ my wild i-deas, _____ but I___

___ do not___ be-lieve that change, can ev-er hap-pen with-out tears. But I

but lov-ing you. _____

Ooh. _____